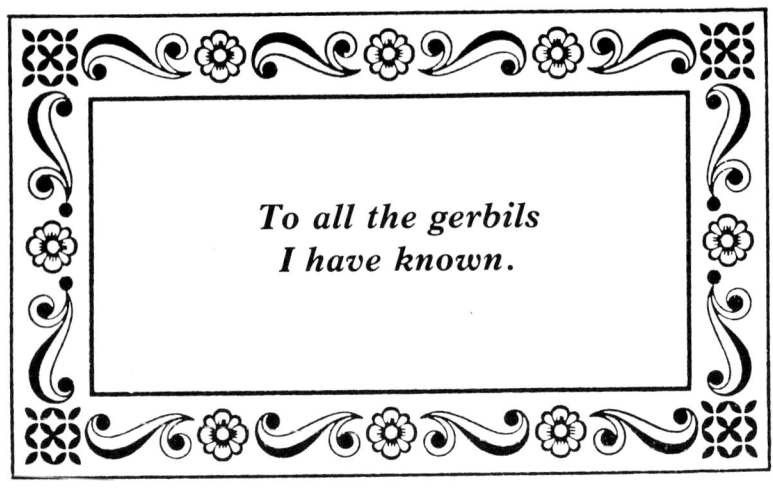

To all the gerbils I have known.

End paper photos by Michael Gilroy.

A Beginners Guide to
Gerbils

Written by
Douglas Keats

Contents

1. **Introduction, 7**
2. **Origin, 11**
3. **Temperament, 15**
   Gerbils are quiet, 17; He sleeps at night, 20
4. **Housing, 21**
   Homemade cages, 23; Keep it clean, 26; Change bedding regularly, 27; Indoors or out, 27
5. **Feeding, 31**
   The diet, 32; Vitamins, 32; Extras, 34
6. **Breeding, 35**
   The first litter, 37; Don't touch, 38; The pair cooperates, 40; Partition, 42
7. **Taming, 43**
   Easy does it, 44; The question of freedom, 45; Two of a kind, 45; The romantic male, 46
8. **Selection, 47**
   The best age, 48; The right sex, 51; Gerbil or Jerbil, 51
9. **Health, 53**
   A healthy gerbil, 54; Good housekeeping, 54; Disinfection, 55; Life span, 56; Sore noses, 58; The coat, 59; Uneaten food, 60

© 1986 by T.F.H. Publications, Inc. Distributed in the UNITED STATES by T.F.H. Publications, Inc., 211 West Sylvania Avenue, Neptune City, NJ 07753; in CANADA by H & L Pet Supplies Inc., 27 Kingston Crescent, Kitchener, Ontario N2B 2T6; Rolf C. Hagen Ltd., 3225 Sartelon Street, Montreal 382 Quebec; in Canada to the Book Trade by Macmillan of Canada (A Division of Canada Publishing Corporation), 164 Commander Boulevard, Agincourt, Ontario M1S 3C7; in ENGLAND by T.F.H. Publications Limited, 4 Kier Park, Ascot, Berkshire SL5 7DS; in AUSTRALIA AND THE SOUTH PACIFIC by T.F.H. (Australia) Pty. Ltd., Box 149, Brookvale 2100 N.S.W., Australia; in NEW ZEALAND by Ross Haines & Son, Ltd., 18 Monmouth Street, Grey Lynn, Auckland 2 New Zealand; in SINGAPORE AND MALAYSIA by MPH Distributors (S) Pte., Ltd., 601 Sims Drive, #03/07/21, Singapore 1438; in the PHILIPPINES by Bio-Research, 5 Lippay Street, San Lorenzo Village, Makati Rizal; in SOUTH AFRICA by Multipet Pty. Ltd., 30 Turners Avenue, Durban 4001. Published by T.F.H. Publications, Inc. Manufactured in the United States of America by T.F.H. Publications, Inc.

1.
Introduction

Recently we stood at a busy pet store counter admiring an attractive display cage filled with Mongolian Gerbils. Having been a gerbil owner for some years, we could not help admiring this healthy, vigorous group.

A dove-colored gerbil in a typical gerbil posture. Photo by Michael Gilroy.

The black gerbil is a female, and the gerbil whose coloration is closer to the wild-colored gerbil is a male—but note the white spot on its head, which denotes it as one of the "Canadian white spot" gerbils. Photo by Michael Gilroy.

Gerbils love to explore house-like and cave-like structures and often make a very appealing picture as they exit. Photo by Michael Gilroy.

Two grandmotherly ladies had stopped to observe the gerbils, and we found ourselves eavesdropping on their conversation. One commented, "They are certainly cute, but what are they? They're not hamsters, these have tails and are smaller; they're not mice or rats, these are prettier, expecially with their tails covered with fur. Besides, their eyes are so large and bright. See how they stand on their hind legs and look out at us!"

It was difficult to control the urge to step in and answer with the typical superiority of a confirmed gerbil-lover, "Of course they're not mice, rats, *or* hamsters, they're 'Super Pets'." However, we realized that they might not quite understand such an enthusiastic statement, so we merely explained that these were recently introduced pets called Mongolian Gerbils, explaining that they have all the virtues of the rodent pet and none of the faults. They are as easy to care for as hamsters but with notably better dispositions. They live together as a family group, with the parents working together to raise their young. They are diurnal, meaning that they are awake during the day, are easily tamed, and love to be handled and petted.

One of the ladies enthusiastically thanked us and said that this was just the pet she had been looking for as a present for her grandson. She purchased a pair of gerbils and asked us dozens of questions about the care and feeding of the new pets, and we answered her questions as best we could.

Later, we realized that other new gerbil owners, too, must have questions, and this book grew from our desire to help.

2. Origin

A gerbil is a small, bright-eyed rodent, similar in appearance to a hamster, although somewhat smaller. His tail is similar in length to that of a mouse, except that the gerbil's tail has a thick covering of golden-brown fur matching that on his body.

Wild gerbils, Meriones unguiculatus, *like the ones shown above are the basic stock from which today's pet gerbils have been derived.*

In some ways gerbils resemble chipmunks, with their bright eyes, their habit of sitting on their haunches, and their insatiable curiosity. The gerbil may walk with the jerky movements of an old-time movie, or because of his elongated back legs he may move in hops or leaps.

A full-grown gerbil weighs less than three ounces and is never more than three or four inches in length. With age, he will put on weight; some of our "elders," the four-year-old group, weigh up to five ounces, but are much less active and playful. One of our gerbils just died, at the age of four years and three months.

There are fourteen known species of gerbil. The particular type in which we are interested is called the Mongolian Gerbil; its scientific name is *Meriones unguiculatus* (family *Cricetidae*). Gerbils are closely related to jerboas and kangaroo rats but are considerably smaller. The correct name for the gerbil is "clawed jird," but gerbil is the more popular name. To confuse the issue further, there have been nine different Latin names assigned to

This male gerbil is "skimming," marking his territory through the use of an oil-secreting gland situated on his abdomen.

Notice how the gerbil's long back feet serve well as balancing mechanisms to allow the animal to adopt an upright posture.

this small mammal. About 1954, the first Mongolian Gerbils were brought to this country from the desert areas of Mongolia. Other species of gerbils are found in the steppes or desert areas from southern Russia and parts of China, India, the Near and Middle East, Mongolia, and into North Africa.

At first, gerbils were imported as laboratory research animals and were used for research on many diseases, including tuberculosis and rickets. Gerbils are still used in lab work, but because of their lovable and placid disposition they have been adopted as pets and for the past five years, they have been bred extensively for this purpose. Profitable breeding has been a difficult task, as little was known at first about the gerbil's living and dietary habits. The gerbil is slightly more expensive than the hamster, domesticated rat or mouse, but the pleasure derived from owning a gerbil is well worth the extra cost. We are learning more about these lovable creatures every day, and as knowledge of them expands and their population increases, their price will decrease.

You'll have fun watching your gerbil explore.

3. Temperament

You will find ownership of this remarkable pet very rewarding in many ways. The gerbil is clean and odorless due, in part, to his diet of seeds and other dry foods. He is affectionate and soon learns to recognize "the hand that feeds him." Readily tamed, he will eat from

A gerbil in a pocket may look cute, but it could be dangerous to the gerbil. Photo by D. G. Robinson, Jr.

Like just about every other rodent, the gerbil is capable of picking objects (potential foodstuffs, mostly) up in its front paws for examination. Photo by Michael Gilroy.

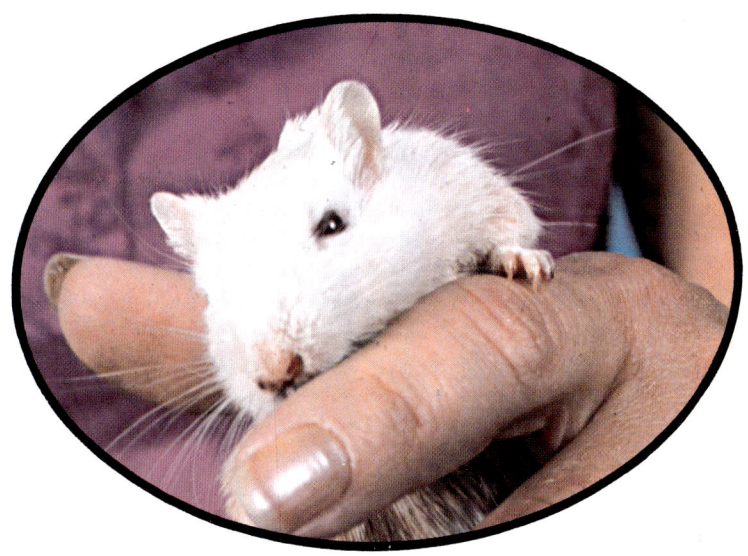

Gerbils can be safely held once they have become accustomed to their owners. Photo by Glen Axelrod.

your hand and enjoy having his back and ears scratched. You will not have long to wait until you may observe both mother and father gerbil caring for the young, as the gestation period (length of pregnancy) is only 23 to 24 days. The gerbil is easy to house and keep clean. His cage or box may be kept in the smallest apartment and, if he is fed the proper diet, neither he nor his droppings have an objectionable odor. He thrives on a diet of seeds and grain, so it is easy to feed him.

Gerbils are quiet

Unlike the squeaker rodents, the gerbil has the smallest of squeaks, so small that you rarely hear it. He does have an unusual and amusing method of communication, and that is "drumming." The male stands on his hind legs to make the drumming sound with his feet. This is usually done when he is frightened, or during mating time when he attempts to attract the female.

Gerbils engage in mutual preening activities that help them to keep clean and socialize with one another. Photo by Michael Gilroy.

This young (21 days old) cinnamon gerbil is rolling a cardboard canister. Pet shops sell gerbil toys that are safer and longer-lasting than makeshift substitutes. Photo by Michael Gilroy.

This albino gerbil is actively sniffing. Photo by R. Hanson.

He sleeps nights

Though he will nap when things are quiet, since he is naturally diurnal, he is awake most of the day. Even at night, when he does most of his sleeping, he is easily awakened. With his boundless energy, wonderful curiosity, placid disposition, and love of people, he is so entertaining that you will pass many a happy hour watching your gerbil play. A pair of gerbils will become very attached to their human companions, enjoying their attention even though they have one another.

Gerbils kept alone make great pets because they are such affectionate creatures that, when deprived of gerbil company, they will be even more dependent on their human companions.

4.
Housing

Whether you use a metal cage such as those sold at your local pet shop, a homemade cage of heavy wood and hardware cloth, or an aquarium tank, make sure that you can observe your gerbils easily and that your gerbils can see you.

Pet shops sell sturdy, easy-to-clean housing units designed to keep gerbils from escaping while also protecting them from other pets in the household. Photo by Vince Serbin.

Inquistive and alert, this gerbil has lifted one of its forefeet in an attitude of watchful curiosity. Photo by D. G. Robinson, Jr.

It's all right to let your gerbils explore a little bit—but don't let them get trapped. Photo by D. G. Robinson, Jr.

You may spend as much or as little money and/or effort as you wish on the cage. At your local pet store there are many types of cages designed specifically for hamsters or gerbils. Most are quite inexpensive, and some are quite elaborate. Cages should have a bottom tray that slides out for easy cleaning. They often come equipped with a running wheel which some gerbils will use and others will not—only the gerbil knows why.

Homemade cages

If you are handy, it is possible to construct a very satisfactory homemade cage. At least one side of the cage should be completely covered with 1/2-inch hardware cloth, and either a side or top door should open wide for easy access. It is a very good idea to line the floor with metal (an old cookie sheet is practical) for ease of cleaning. Though gerbils will not gnaw as diligently as hamsters (gerbils seem more contented with their surroundings so long as they are kept clean and well fed), they can and do gnaw, so be sure that all wood used is good and thick. Some people prefer to line the bottom with hardware cloth, but the gerbil is happier and more comfortable on a solid floor covered with clean bedding.

A square aquarium is very satisfactory housing for your gerbil; you can see him from all sides, and it is so easy to clean. It can be anywhere from five gallons up, depending on the size of your gerbil family. It is usually possible to obtain a second-hand aquarium or a "leaker" at a reduced price from a pet shop.

The choice of cover again depends on what you wish to spend. Pet shops stock metal hoods that fit the tops of most aquariums, or you can make a cover with 1/4- or 1/2-inch hardware cloth. Bend it down at the corners with a pliers to fit over the top like a box lid. It is rare for a gerbil to "break out." When he does he usually returns on his own, but the lid is a safety factor, keeping the gerbil in and other family pets out.

A large glass jar may be used, provided it has enough floor space so the gerbils can move around, as they need exercise and love to romp and play. In addition to the exercise wheel, give your pets a log or a piece of untreated wood. They will spend hours chewing, climbing, and playing hide-and-seek on it. They will also enjoy a tin can that has been opened on both ends to serve as a tunnel.

This black female gerbil is heavily pregnant, as can be seen from the abdominal bulge. Photo by Michael Gilroy.

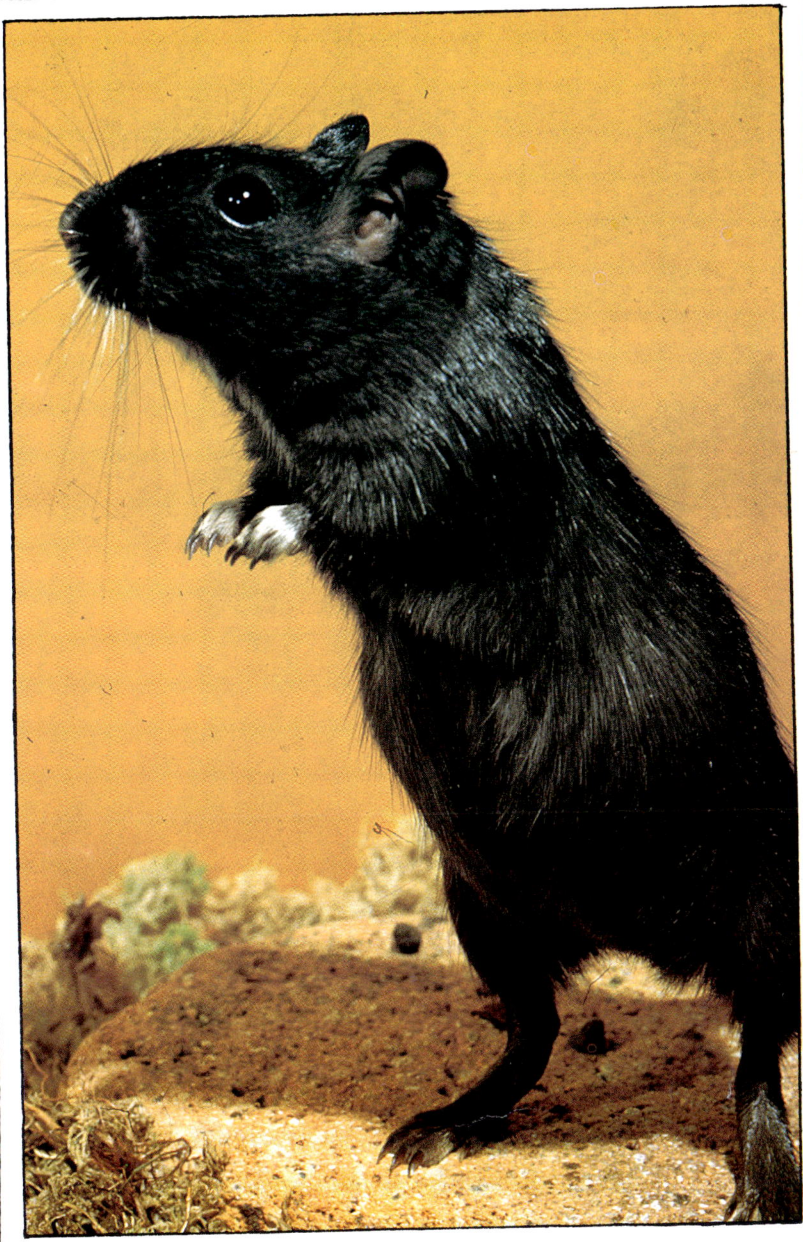

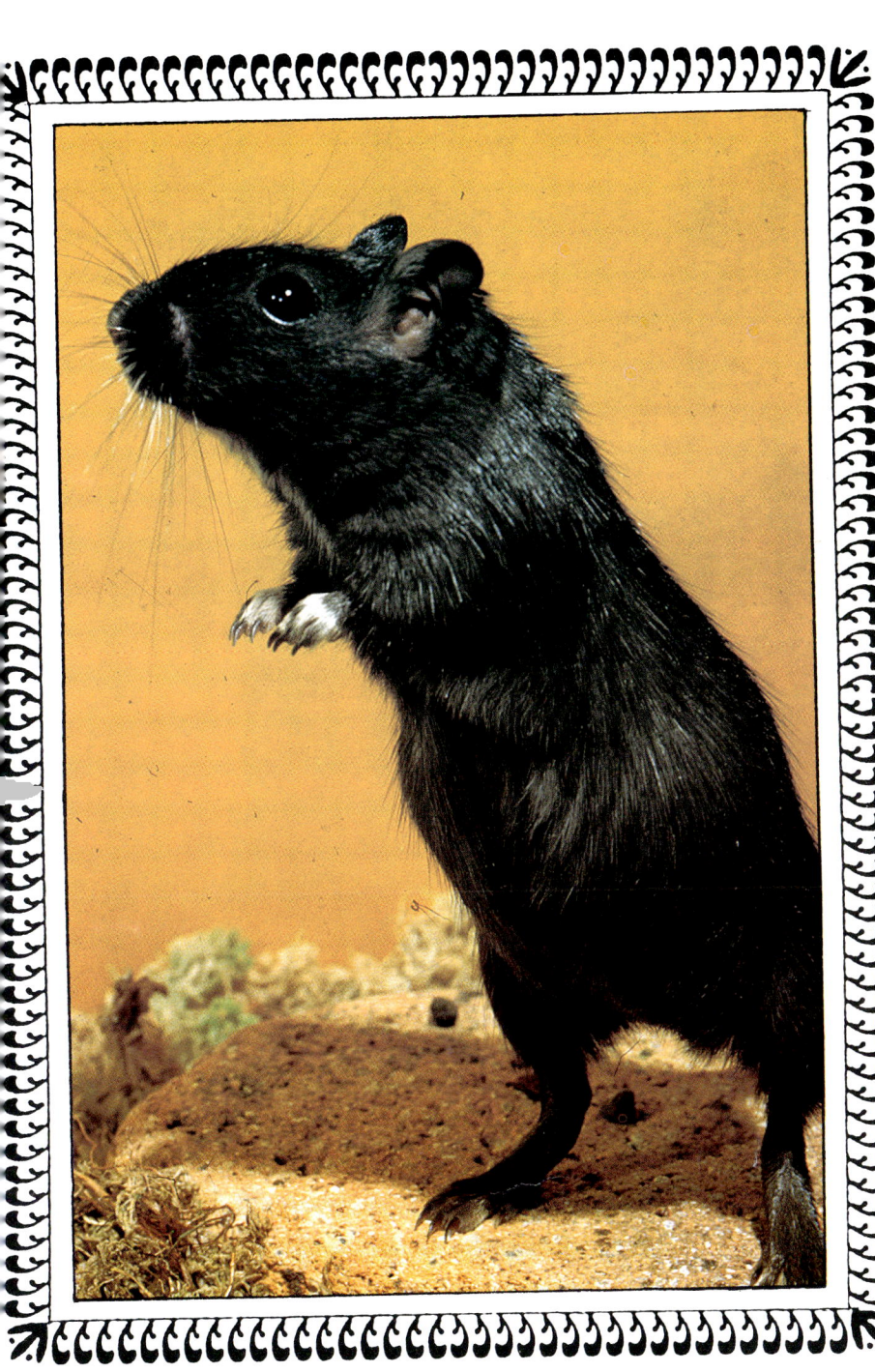

Gerbils tend to get heavier as they get older, and the extra weight can hurt them, so watch their diet. Photo by D. G. Robinson, Jr.

Keep it clean

The most important consideration, whatever housing you decide on, is that the cage be clean and dry. Commercially packed cedar chips treated with chlorophyll are a very satisfactory covering for the floor of the cage. They are inexpensive, and the gerbils enjoy sharpening their teeth on the chips. You may obtain wood shavings from your local lumber yard, use sand or kitty litter, or even newspapers. The gerbil sems to have a good time tearing newspapers to build a nest, though papers seem to soil quicker and need changing more often than other types of bedding. There is a question though as to whether the gerbil may be harmed by the ink in the newsprint. A very satisfactory and economical bedding is small 3 x 3 inch squares of burlap bag, and it is amazing to watch the gerbil tear these up, ending with fluffy bedding that looks as though it's made of downy brown cotton.

Even though we use cedar chips in all our cages, we give burlap to our pregnant females for nest making. Gerbils are creatures of habit, and some of our older gerbils who have had nothing but cedar chips will completely ignore the burlap, but when the cedar chips are removed the gerbils make use of the burlap. It seems that humans are not the only creatures spoiled by "modern conveniences."

Change bedding regularly

With only two gerbils (and a young family) in a cage, it is necessary to completely clean the cage only about once a month. Empty all the bedding, wash and dry the cage thoroughly, and provide new clean bedding. We add a few new cedar chips about once a week. The gerbils are always very excited over fresh ones which also serve to freshen whatever odor the cage may have. We also check to see that there is no excess food in the cage.

Many breeders advocate supplying hay, as both bedding and a dietary supplement. In the wild, gerbils live in deep burrows in the ground, and though we have never tried it, they would probably enjoy a layer of sand and chips to burrow under, provided the cage is deep enough.

Indoors or out

You will probably want to keep your gerbils indoors, but if you wish you may keep them outside, so long as the cage is sheltered from the elements and from direct sunlight. The temperature should be moderate; they

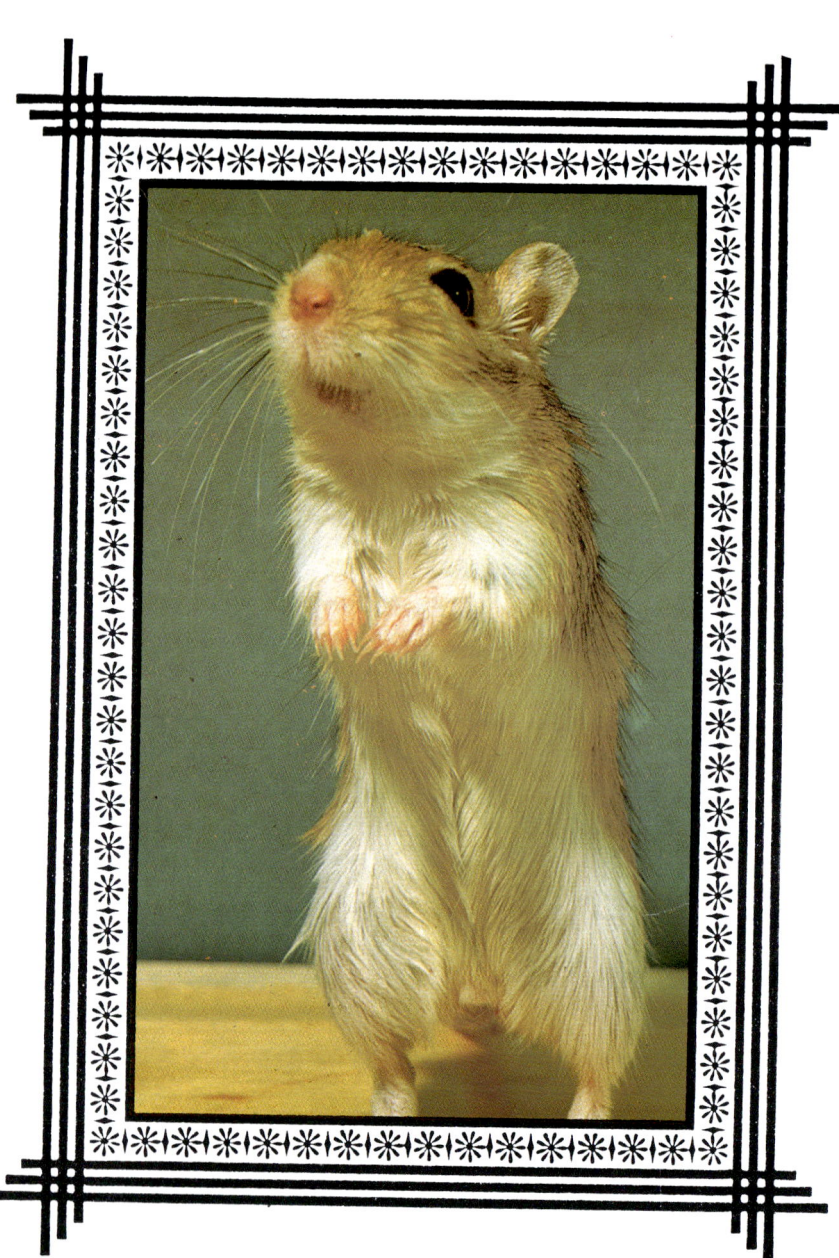

Gerbils aren't above begging for tidbits—and how can you resist them? Photo by Michael Gilroy.

Gerbil babies three weeks of age. Photo by Michael Gilroy.

Under certain circumstances a gerbil could easily be confused with a mouse. Photo by Sally Anne Thompson.

like warm days and cool nights. They are less active in cold weather, and if they are outdoors they should be provided with an extra amount of bedding. Gerbils are less active during extremely hot *or* cold weather and are happiest and healthiest when the temperature is between 45 and 85F.

5. Feeding

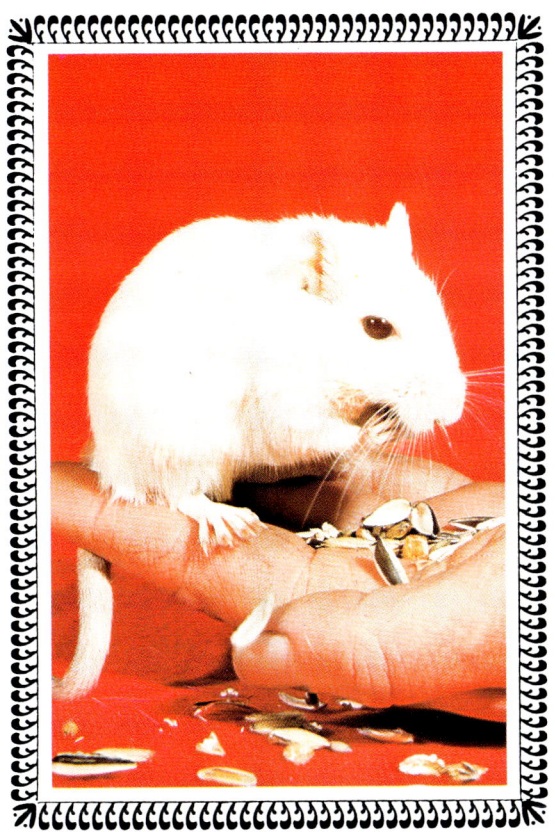

In his natural habitat, the gerbil lives on seeds, grasses, roots and grains. In desert country, where there is little drinking water available, he probably gets the water necessary for his body functions from the dew and the grasses. Though the gerbil does not take a large amount

Gerbils like to eat sunflower seeds, but no one food should be fed to the exclusion of all others. Photo by R. Hanson.

of water, it should be available at all times. It is important to keep his cage dry, as he is always tipping a bowl of water or filling it with his bedding. The best system is a gravity water dispenser, also known as a suck bottle fastened to the side of his cage. These are available inexpensively at any pet store. Most of the time it seems that he drinks nothing, while at other times two gerbils will wrestle for possession of the bottle. A great deal more water is drunk during hot weather, so care should be taken to see that the bottle is filled at all times.

The diet

A diet of sunflower seeds and kibbled dog or cat food is nutritionally satisfactory and is easily provided for the gerbil in captivity. The kibbled food has the vitamin and food supplements he needs, while the sunflower seeds are rich in fats (47%) and proteins (24.3%). This diet alone is sufficient, and most commercial breeders are satisfied with the breeding results obtained when this diet is fed. Some breeders supplement the diet with grains such as wheat, barley, oats, millet, canary seed, and even watermelon or pumpkin seeds. Gerbils seem to like apples; feed only small bits. Fresh seeding grasses are especially beneficial.

A tablespoon or two of food a day per gerbil is enough.

Vitamins

There are some differences of opinion as to the necessity for supplementing the diet with vitamins. We feel that they are not necessary if a well-balanced diet is being fed. However, they do no harm, so if in doubt, by all means purchase a supply from your pet dealer. Always follow label directions carefully.

This gerbil appears to be guarding its supply of sunflower seeds and looks prepared to fight off all potential seed thieves. Photo by D. G. Robinson, Jr.

Greenfoods may be given on occasion as special treats, but don't load up your gerbil's diet with fresh greens in the mistaken belief that they're good for him. Photo by D. G. Robinson, Jr.

Extras

If you find a great deal of leftover food in the cage, it means that you are overfeeding. Gerbils, like all living creatures, enjoy a treat such as peanuts and potato chips once in a while, though we don't advise feeding these often. Individual gerbils develop a fondness for particular foods. Lettuce, carrots and other fresh vegetables are not particularly good for the gerbil. Stick to the grain and kibbled food diet, and you will have a cleaner cage. Feed your gerbil what he *needs* first and, after he has eaten, offer treats as a dessert.

6. Breeding

If you wish to breed your gerbil, ask your dealer to help you pick a male and a female. The male has a more pointed posterior and the scrotal pouch is usually dark in color. The female's body is rounder and the genital opening is closer to the anal opening.

Baby gerbils in the nest with their mother. Photo by D. G. Robinson, Jr.

A black mother gerbil and her one-day-old babies. Not every female gerbil is a good mother to her babies. Photo by Michael Gilroy.

The first litter

What delightful excitement for you and your family when the female produces her first litter, and what a wonderful education to watch Mama and Daddy gerbil share in the care. The gestation or pregnancy period is about 24 days and there may be anywhere from one to six babies, though the average litter is four to six. The babies are hairless, and their pink skin is almost transparent. The eyes stay closed for about three weeks, but the stronger ones will start crawling out of the nest by the end of the first week. By this time they have a fine fuzz growing on their bodies. At three weeks of age they are covered with red-gold hair, their eyes are open, and they are miniature replicas of their parents.

This baby gerbil's eyes still have not opened, as he's still only about two weeks old. Photo by D. G. Robinson, Jr.

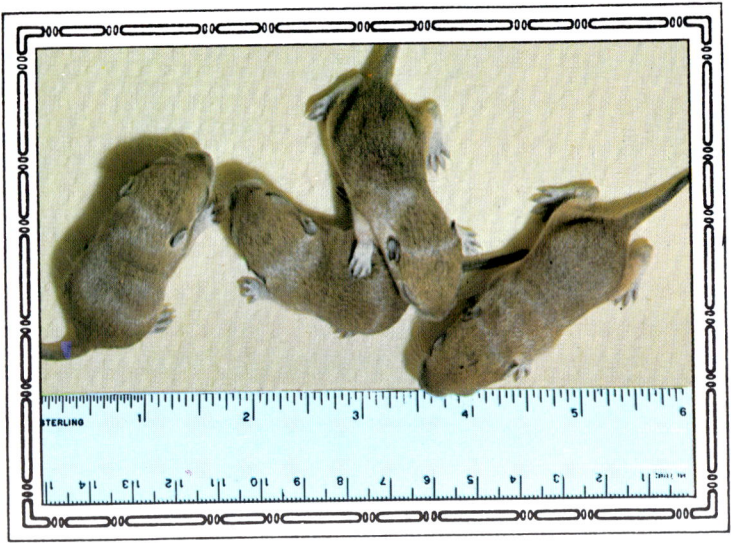

The two-week-old gerbils shown here can be matched against the ruler to get an idea of their size at this age; the graduations on the ruler are in inches. Photo by D. G. Robinson, Jr.

Don't touch

For most litters, the rule is *do not touch* until the eyes are open. The tamest of females is often very nervous. She will move the babies from place to place in her cage, each time carefully covering them with the nesting material, but don't worry, she will uncover them later. She often leaves the father to mind them while she is eating or drinking. Mothers with unusually large litters may divide the litter and place a few in each corner of the cage. It shows her intelligence, as there will be less competition between siblings during the nursing period. The mother weans the babies when they are five or six weeks of age. If the male has been with her during this period, likely as not she is already expecting another litter. The babies will eat solid food as soon as their eyes are open, even though they are still nursing.

This mature Canadian white spot male and his dove-colored mate are preening. Preening is not necessarily sex-related. Photo by Michael Gilroy.

Gerbils can be trained to eat from your hand if you exercise patience. Photo by R. Hanson.

The saddest question to answer is, "Why does my female let her young die, or sometimes even kill or eat them?" Unfortunately, there is no one answer, nor do we know all of the answers. First of all, the mother is naturally protective and nervous, so *if* there is a lot of noise, *if* you touch the newborn babies, *if* her diet is not well-balanced, or *if* she is bickering with her mate, she may kill or neglect her young. *If* she has been bred too frequently she may not have enough milk and the young will die.

The pair cooperates

Make sure the gerbils have clean, fresh bedding before the babies arrive, *then leave them alone*. Keep them in a quiet spot, and no matter how tempted you are, please resist peeking at the babies, or the mother will become upset. This may be the time to offer the mother a little milk, although some will not take it. It is more practical to mix dry powdered milk (in very small amounts) with the dry food during her pregnancy and nursing period. It is rare for the male to upset the mother, especially if they have been kept together. Usually, he is as concerned with the babies as she is. He functions as an excellent "baby sitter," both literally and figuratively, as he usually sits on them to keep them warm while the mother is away, eating and exercising.

If the male does seem to be bothering the newborn babies, or if the female seems to resent him, remove him from the cage. If possible, though, it is better to leave him in the cage with a hardware cloth partition placed between him and his family. This way, he can become accustomed to the young without being able to harm them. By the time they have their eyes open you may return the father to the community, to help with the adolescents. This is the time babies are at their cutest and never seem to tire of romping and playing.

This gerbil is not well; a sick gerbil should not be used for breeding. Photo by D. G. Robinson, Jr.

This attentive mother is ministering to three of her babies. Photo by D. G. Robinson, Jr.

Partitions

The use of the hardware cloth partition in the same cage is also most practical when two gerbils do not "take" to one another immediately. After a few days in the same cage, they can be put together safely. We know we will receive letters from readers telling of their mother gerbil who allows the babies to be handled right from birth. We have had several such mothers, but these are the exceptions rather than the rule, so best play safe until you are sure how the new mother will react.

7.
Taming

"Do unto others, etc." simply means that you should show someone else the same courtesies you expect in return, and this holds true for your treatment of your pets as well. While every hamster authority tells you that a new hamster is a nervous hamster and to watch your fingers when you handle him, this admonition is

The degree of success you have in training a gerbil is greatly dependent on how well the animal has been treated and how susceptible to handling it is. Photo by D. G. Robinson, Jr.

rare with the gerbil because he is not at all nervous by nature. While he may scurry away from your hand, when you do pick him up he will rarely bite unless he is—or has been—mistreated. Gentle, and his curiosity often exceeding his fear, he may even run up to your hand the moment you place it in the cage. A gerbil will never charge at your hand with the intention of biting, but when handling a new gerbil do not poke or squeeze him. As with any strange animal, it is best to extend a closed fist because he may nip an extended finger, thinking it is something you are offering to eat. It is a good idea to have a bit of food in your palm and open your hand slowly to let him find it. Thus, he will associate your hand with his favorite occupation—eating. The most satisfactory gerbil to tame is one which is newly weaned. Weanlings seem to have no fear, and they look to you for the comfort previously received from their family.

Easy does it

While the gerbil is inspecting your hand or eating from it, gently scratch his back and ears. He will soon learn to relax, and this is the time to start handling him. Whatever your reason for picking him up, whether to remove him for cage cleaning or just for cuddling him it is always safest (at first) to pick him up by the tail, close to his body. Gerbils move very fast and can be injured by leaping from your hand, so place him in your hand and cup it gently around his body. Do not squeeze him, but talk to him quietly and rub his back. If he is very active, continue to hold onto his tail while he is in your hand. Until a child becomes accustomed to handling gerbils, it may be a good idea to have him sit on a couch or some similar place where a jump or fall will not injure your gerbil.

This is a dwarf gerbil of the genus Gerbillus; *successful hybridizations between this species and the Mongolian gerbil have not been made.*

The question of freedom

The question of allowing gerbils their freedom in the home is often raised. While it is true that gerbils will learn to return to their cage just as they return to the home burrow in nature, the hazards of a home are so great that complete unsupervised freedom cannot be recommended. Among the hazards which might be listed are rodent traps, fresh paint, insect poisons, open doors or windows leading outside the house, stray cats or dogs, visitors who might inadvertently step on them, and the chance that they might slip or fall into a location from which they cannot escape.

Two of a kind

If you do not wish to breed your gerbil but would still like to have more than one, two females do best together and get along fine. Two males that have been raised in a community litter situation nearly always get along well, too. *Rarely* can you put together two males that have once been mated, even if they have been together up until that time. One will kill the other, although there are always exceptions. We know of one gerbil "family" which consists of one full-grown female living with two males, and all three are very happy. Both males even help with the newborn babies. This is rare, as the gerbil social situation is much like that of the human's; that is, for the most part they are monogamous. Often, when a couple has been together over a long period and one mate dies, the other will not accept a new mate readily. The widow or widower, as the case may be, will just ignore the proffered new mate or may even fight with the newcomer. But time heals all wounds, and eventually their desire for companionship prevails and they accept the new mate.

The romantic male

It is true that if you are short of males, some of them may be passed from one female to the other. However, in discussing this procedure with commercial breeders, we have found that they are wary of the system. If you should move a male or a female to a new mate, watch the pair carefully and separate them at the first sign of belligerence. Here again, a screen divider may be profitably employed for several days. Safely divided, they can gradually become accustomed to the odor and presence of the new mate.

We have one male who must be a true rodent Casanova. We have passed him around among the females and he goes happily from one to the other, with no difficulty on either side. He even stays on to help with the new family, but moves on willingly when the times comes. This is a rarity, but perhaps he is just not ready to "settle down."

8. Selection

Gerbils are relatively disease-free, so if you find one that does not have a plump firm body, bright eyes and energy-plus, it means he has been improperly fed and cared for.

Gerbils are hardy animals and don't require much special care, so they can be maintained in good health easily enough—but make sure that you choose a healthy animal to begin with.

Watch as the gerbil dealer takes him from the cage. He will either panic and dart away or run to the dealer's hand. Whatever he does, he will not stay still. A healthy gerbil is always active, and unless he is sleeping he is never still. If he is sleeping, he is easily awakened. If he is lethargic, he is ill. His fur should be thick and luxurious. Due to the gerbil's placid disposition, most dealers keep them together in a cage.

The best age

The ideal time to acquire your pet is, as previously mentioned, just after the gerbil has been weaned, about six weeks of age. If a female is more than two months old and has been living in a community cage, and if you are not interested in raising a family, you had better settle for a male. She might surprise you with a litter a short time after she moves in. If your female should present you with an unexpected litter, don't panic; feed her

Safely cradled in their owner's arms, these gerbils are completely comfortable. Photo by D. G. Robinson, Jr.

This excellent closeup shows a gerbil at its best, sparkling with vitality and alertness. Photo by Michael Gilroy.

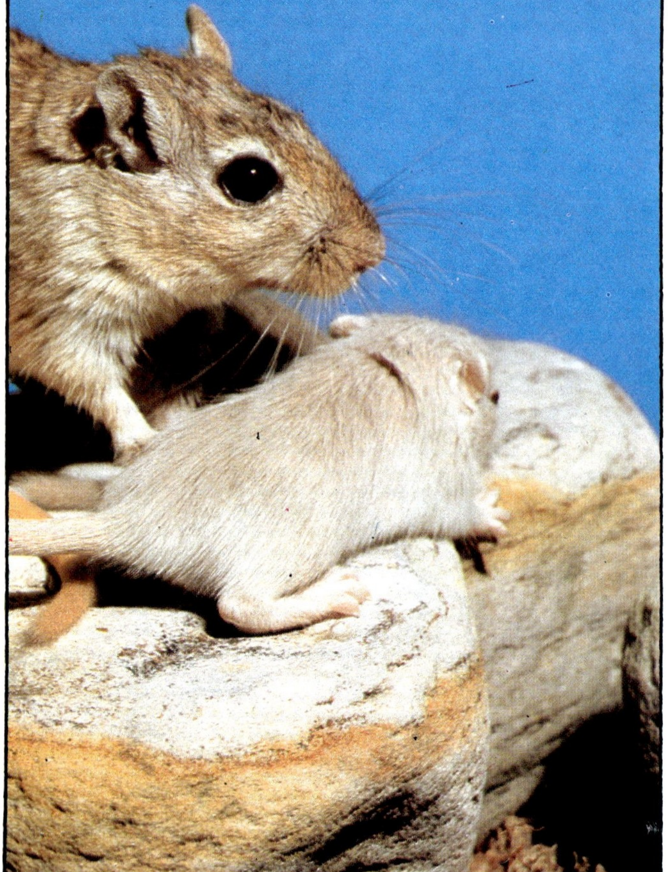

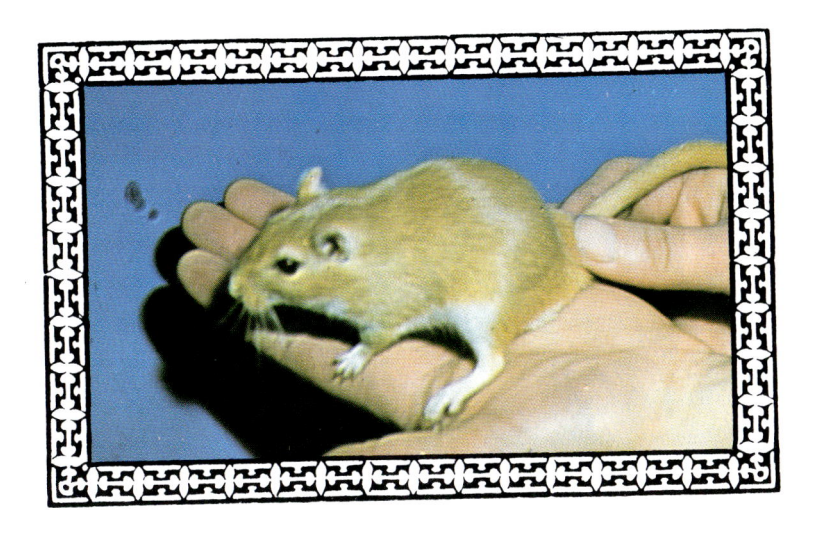

Facing page: Here a male gerbil oversees his offspring. Photo by Michael Gilroy. *Above:* This gerbil is being correctly held at the base of its tail. Photo by R. Hanson.

well, give her plenty of water, and she will do the rest. The babies are no trouble, and your local pet shop may take the unwanted babies off your hands the minute they are old enough.

The right sex

As for the sex to select, both female and male are equally placid. The female will sometimes be more nervous when she is expecting or nursing, but this is natural.

Gerbil or Jerbil

There is a certain amount of confusion about the proper pronunciation for gerbil. Some zoologists, pet shop owners, and breeders pronounce the word with a hard *g*; while others prefer a soft *j* sound. If the professionals

51

Regardless of how you pronounce its name, the gerbil is deservedly a popular pet.

cannot agree, probably the average layman is as unsure of the pronunciation as we are. Actually, both are correct; it just depends on which you prefer. Eventually one pronunciation will be selected as correct through popular usage. One of the early Latin names, given years ago in the *Encyclopedia Britannica,* was *Gerbillus aegytiacus.* Because the average scientist pronounces Latin *g*'s as a soft *j* sound, we might assume that gerbil would be pronounced *j*erbil. However, since German is often the language of modern science, the Europeans pronounce it with a hard *g*—gerbil.

Since the *g* in Mongolian is certainly the hard *g* sound, it seems easier to say Mongolian Gerbil, with a hard *g* in both words. But say it as you like, and either one will be correct.

9. Health

The gerbil is naturally healthy, so there is usually little to worry about. Unlike most small mammals, he is not particularly prone to colds or pneumonia. In fact, in their natural state they have no known diseases. Since gerbils today have been bred in captivity for generations, there is no danger of rabies.

A gerbil with a serious illness will give evidence of its sickness, becoming listless and apathetic, much unlike this perky little fellow. Photo by Michael Gilroy.

A healthy gerbil

A healthy gerbil has a sleek coat, his eyes are bright and he is interested in everything that goes on about him. A sick gerbil will huddle in the corner, his coat will look rough and he will respond sluggishly. This seldom happens if he is kept clean, dry and draft free.

Good housekeeping

See that your pet is fed a balanced and sensible diet, has a clean dry home, and is not exposed to extreme temperatures. High temperatures do not bother him, provided he is in the shade. Soft foods, citrus, or raw meat are not advisable because they may cause diarrhea. Also, raw meat may induce him to develop a taste for his roommate. It cannot be too often repeated that the diet for your gerbil is dry foods, grains, seeds, and kibbled pet food. There is a special mix for hamsters which may be fed to gerbils. Although it is slightly more expensive, it will agree with him.

Don't experiment with exotic foods in your gerbil's diet; pet gerbils do best on a good pelleted food designed for gerbils. Photo by Michael Gilroy.

A mouse and gerbil shown together for purposes of comparison. Although animals such as these that are raised together probably will get along well, there is not much to be gained by mixing them. Photo by Paul Bartley.

Do not bathe your pet gerbil. He spends many hours grooming and combing his fur and tail with his five-fingered paws. He is very clean.

Disinfection

Vermin thrive in a dirty cage. Should this happen, wash the cage thoroughly, using a good disinfectant. Dust your gerbil with a cat flea powder or one sold for hamsters. Gerbils, like cats and hamsters, lick themselves and, therefore, only a powder which is not toxic when ingested may be used. This problem will rarely arise, and if he comes from a clean environment and you see that his quarters are kept clean and dry, you will not be troubled at all.

Life span

The gerbil's productive period is about two years. His life span in captivity is between three and four years. An elderly couple of gerbils, past their productive years, is best left together. They are touchingly affectionate with one another and thrive best when left with their accustomed mates.

Occasionally, they will produce later than two years, but then the litters will be smaller. Also, the older female may neglect her young, probably because she does not have enough milk for them.

Facing page: These gerbils exhibit the freshness of youth—but they'll still be enjoyable pets even after they've aged considerably. Photo by Michael Gilroy.
Below: Young or old, a gerbil will give its owner much pleasure if handled with the consideration that it's entitled to. Photo by Sally Anne Thompson.

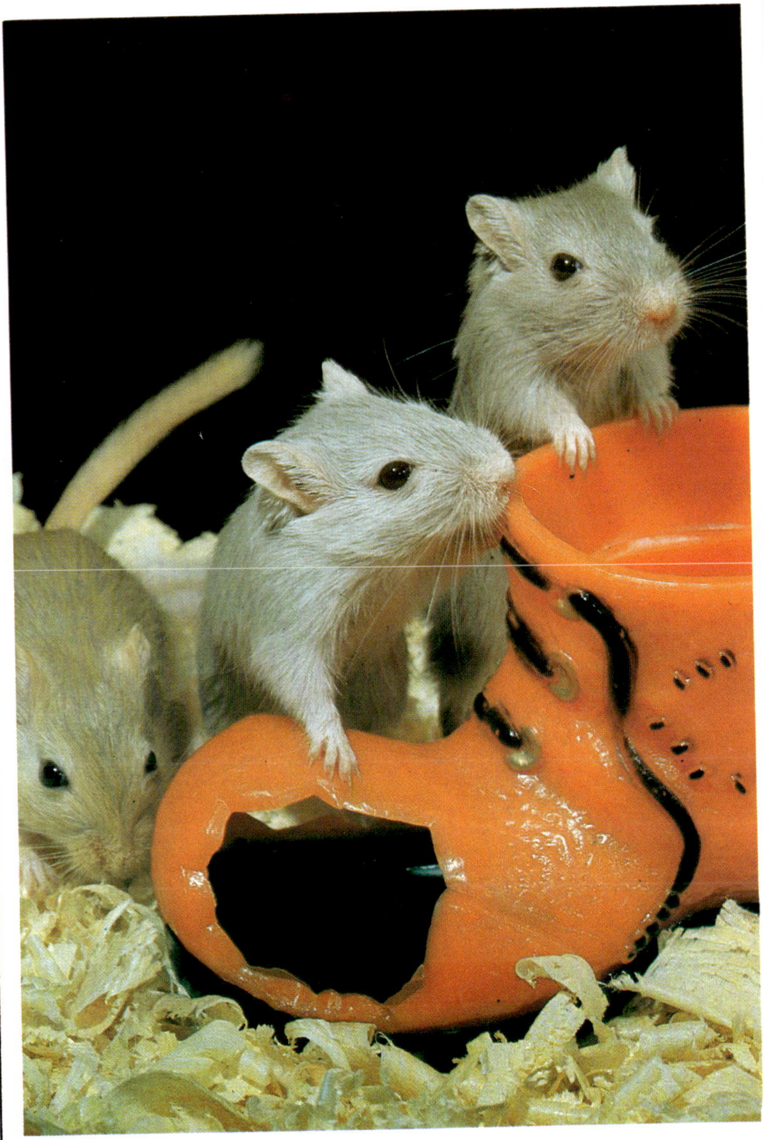

Sore noses

Gerbil owners frequently ask what to do about sore noses on their pet. Most of them explain that they are keeping the cages clean and feeding a complete diet. Of course, one assumes that an owner conscientious enough to bother inquiring is concerned enough to keep his gerbil clean and well fed. Treat the nose with an antibiotic ointment available in your pet shop, and add supplemental vitamins to his diet. Para-aminobenzoic acid,

Occasional checks on the appearance of a pet gerbil and its behavior will help to ward off potential health problems. Photo by Michael Gilroy.

The color of the coat is of no great significance as a barometer of health, but the condition of the coat is. Photo by R. Hanson.

known as PABA, is one of the vitamin B complex and may prove helpful. It is available in tablets which are easily crushed. A little of the powder may then be mixed with the food. If treatment does not help, try changing the bedding. If you have been using cedar chips, try the burlap or even a sandy bottom on the cage for a while. If clean sand is not available, kitty litter will serve the same purpose. We do not advise using newspaper, as most newsprint inks have toxic properties which may irritate the nose. Since gerbils react like humans in so many respects, your pet may be allergic to something which is tolerated by the average gerbil. If he is living with a mate or in a community cage, it may be a good idea to isolate him for a while until you can determine what is causing the condition.

The coat

A healthy gerbil has thick hair, a protective sandy coloration like the desert countries from which he comes. When you brush the hair back it is rather a surprise to discover that the undercoating is slate gray. The outer hair is so thick the gray does not show through. Most of our gerbils have black guard hairs scattered among the gold. These are just long enough to give the illusion of being black tips on the fur and only close inspection shows that they are separate hairs.

Uneaten food

Some gerbils after they have eaten what they need for the day store the food remaining in one corner of the cage. Give them a little less food daily, and the cage will be fresher. Gerbils do not have pouches in their cheeks for storing food, but munch very fast while holding the food in their front paws.

As mentioned at the beginning of this book, you will find ownership of this remarkable pet very rewarding.

In a bare transport cage such as shown below leftovers would be very easy to spot, but in a cage equipped with shavings (facing page) they'd be less detectable. Photo by Michael Gilroy.

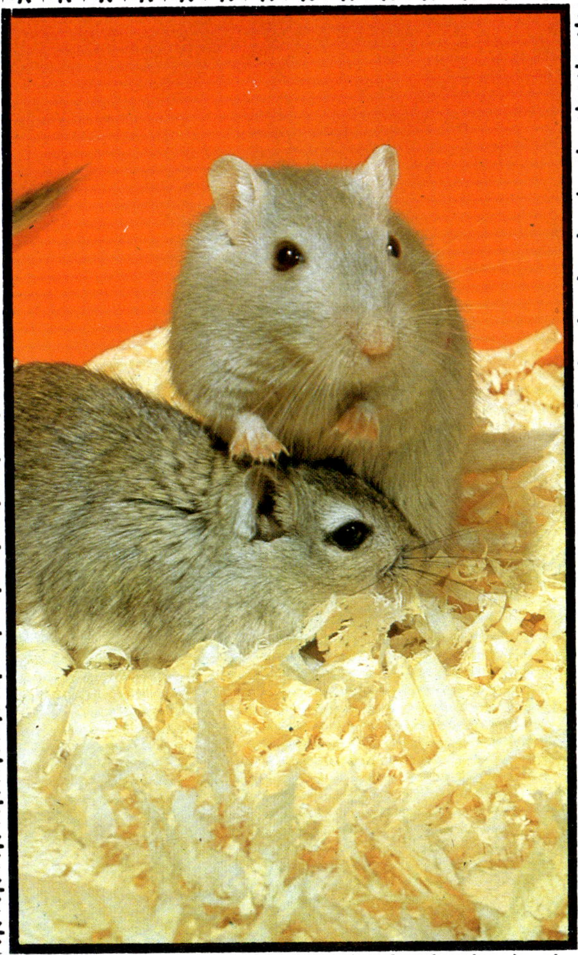